IMMIGRANT

IMMIGRANT

USHA KISHORE

EYEWEAR PUBLISHING

First published in 2018
by Eyewear Publishing Ltd
Suite 333, 19-21 Crawford Street
Marylebone, London W1H 1PJ
United Kingdom

Cover design and typeset by Edwin Smet
Author photograph by Isle of Man Newspapers

Printed in England by TJ International Ltd, Padstow, Cornwall

ISBN 978-1-912477-08-1

MIX
Paper from
responsible sources
FSC® C013056

This publication has been supported by Culture Vannin (Isle of Man)

WWW.EYEWEARPUBLISHING.COM

For the *khanabadosh* of the world,
who, like me, are eternal wanderers...

Usha Kishore
is an Indian-born British poet
and translator, resident on the Isle of Man.
Her poetry has been internationally published and
anthologised by Macmillan, Hodder Wayland, Oxford
University Press, Harper Collins India and Orient
BlackSwan. Kishore's poetry is part of the British
primary and Indian middle school and undergraduate
syllabi. She won the Pre-Raphaelite Poetry Prize (2013),
Exiled Writers Ink Poetry Competition (2014), and the
Word Masala Award (2016). Kishore is the author
of two previous poetry collections and a book of
translation from the Sanskrit.

TABLE OF CONTENTS

Come, come, whoever you are,
Wanderer, worshipper, lover of leaving. It doesn't matter.
Ours is not a caravan of despair.

– Rumi

ABSENT SKY

Manasarovar

Snow dyes the mind, freezing the myth
of time. Passing clouds wax astral batiks
into the fabric of still air, *mandalas*

and *yantras* for wandering souls.
Thought translates into blue eternity,
veiling the kneeling earth in immortal hue.

In the paling distance, on a mist-clad
rock dome, jewelled in glacial ice,
a celestial being, wearing the crescent moon

on his forehead, contemplates the world.
Day and night merge into cosmic dreams
as winds gasp between sound and silence.

Rainbow flags flutter in tranquil prayer
and a twilight *mantra* rises on wings of fire,
as the mind lake meditates on an absent sky.

JOURNEYING INTO A FOREIGN TONGUE

Journeying into a foreign tongue
is like re-incarnating yourself
in an unknown form.

I don't need passports and visas
to journey into a foreign tongue,
I just need to lose myself in it.

I line up my Hindu gods,
adorned in monsoon winds
and trespass into English verse.

A new horizon opens, and I
dressed in borrowed robes,
journey into a foreign tongue.

A child, holding the hand of postcoloniality...

POSTCOLONIAL POEM

You are the enterprising seafarer,
in search of adventure.

I am the wild orient, waiting
to be discovered.

You cast your imperial net.
I welcome you like a god.

You trade. You invade.
You conquer. You divide.

I bleed in saffron and green. I sing
patriotic songs in mumbo-jumbo.

You exorcise my pagan spirit
with cross and book.

You teach me your language.
I curse in your language.

I unite. I shout slogans.
I subvert. I burn you down.

Your guns thunder down.
I die. But I rise again.

You imprison me. You call me
traitor, in the name of the crown.

I engage in non-violence. I desire truth.
I non co-operate. I fast unto death.

My swelling masses flood you out.
Your sun is set. You saw me in two.

Yet, I rise again. I build nations.
You seek new horizons.

We pretend to ignore each other.
But we need each other.

I dream of the western skies.
You dream of a new empire.

I come. I see. I conquer.
I teach you your language.

Together, we journey through Prospero-land.
My pagan spirit resurrects in mumbo-jumbo.

I people your island with little Calibans.
You hurl abuse. You discriminate.

I resist. You make new laws.
I teach you my language.

You mumble my name
in your colonial tongue.

I AM NOT ONE, BUT TWO

A swallow flies into the sky,
penetrates the blue and returns
with a *chakora* bird. The swallow
takes me in its beak, flies
to a waiting flock in the horizon
and spits me out. The *chakora* bird
picks me up, takes me to its nest
in the rainbow and drops me
into the sea. They fight over me,
for I am half swallow, half *chakora*.
I am not one, but two. I live
on both sides of the sky,
I fly in and out of the blue,
I sing with my forked tongue
of strange new worlds and
stranger ways. I have no flock,
no music, no culture,
for I am not one but two.
I am half swallow, half *chakora*.
But I am not lost, I am not alone,
I am not afraid. My past seeps
into my present; my future,
a strange mixture of magic
and realism. I am not one but two.
India bleeds in my veins; England
paints my feathers with her mists.

YOU AND ME

You woo my votes and visit my temples
and mosques. You wear my red *tilak*
on your forehead, my flower garlands
around your neck. You knock at my door
to ask for more votes and do a disappearing act
when I speak of integration. You say that you believe
in the brotherhood of man and quietly graffiti
your white walls with charcoal: *Paki, go home* –
not knowing that *pak* means pure.
You moan at unpronounceable foreign names
and preach multiculturalism. I teach Steve Biko
and Maya Angelou to your children, who write notes
of apology: *Sorry for showing racism to you, Miss.*

You admire my Benares silk *saris*, my ethnic
silver jewellery and smile at my love for your poetry.
I write my dissertations on equal Rights,
you nod approval. At lunch time, we discuss
Jabberwocky and Godot, my Indian thoughts
fire your British hearts, something in your
Englishness warms my Malayali soul.

And in the mornings, I cut across the A2
and think of you and me, beating in time to
Kula Shaker's *Radha Ramana Hare, Hare…*

POSTCOLONIAL SONNET

I do not have a language to claim as my own
only an irrevocable parental pledge made
on the pyre of a deceased empire to dye me
in the colours of invading eloquence; ubiquitous
force that even time cannot conquer. Island-born
linguistic code mapping out its domain on land,
sea and air; accent and dialect spreading like wildfire.
An imperial dream to enrich, to educate, to engender
vehicles of superior literary expression; a civilising
mission advancing through meandering rivers
and majestic railroads to monopolise over rude,
indigenous vernaculars. Restive, my thoughts
wait in the wings to appropriate the colonial tongue
and versify a postcolonial *Weltanschauung*.

IN-BETWEEN SPACE

The red of the morning contouring itself
on the black of the night, a chiaroscuro dawn,
baring her vermillion bosom to the rising sun.

A night flight between two continents, turning
into light somewhere over brooding desert skies,
where the drifting mind soars on falcon wings.

You have dreamt between distracted archipelagos,
floundering coral reefs and lost peninsulas, hitching
dragon rides in a world of camels and elephants.

You have mapped cultural spaces with crepuscular icons
of demons and demiurges churning immortal serpents
in the misty oceans of the milky way. You have lived

in fear of Jupiter's thunderbolt and Indra's *vajra*, gathering
gemstone legends from the lands you traversed in search
of a dark eternity. You have inherited the scent of jasmine

flowers, the loss of womanhood hanging on pomegranate
trees and the fate of the ever-wandering *khanabadosh*.
Lounging on the peacock throne of in-between space,

you sip cloudy twilight from a tall glass and fathom
the sensuous curve of the sky as it meets the sea.
Blinded by the light of the rising sun, you lose time

in a kaleidoscope of bewildered geographies, each
glass bead, flowering as second, minute and hour.
Now, it is landing time – you stretch, fold away

the blanket of sleep, apply your *kajal* and lip gloss
and tune into the dulcet tones of a language that melts
into turquoise sea and emerald palm fronds.

BASTARD CHILDREN OF THE BRITISH RAJ

What shall we call ourselves?
Diaspora, self-exiles, immigrants,
bastard children of the British Raj?
We wander everywhere and anywhere:
the musical sites of Vienna, London's
multicultural streets, the subways
of Paris, the waterways of Venice,
carrying our hyperbolic worlds,
brimming with *masala chai*, overflowing
with sequinned *saris* and a certain longing
for home that does not exist anymore.
Lost souls, we contemplate border crossings
in continents that spill over us, in passports
that do not share our skin colour.
We cruise down the Thames, shop for
souvenirs on the Champs Élysées, catch
the leaning tower of Pisa in our sleep,
write poetry on the Isle of Man, circle
the world, longing for childhoods
lived in exotic locations.
We are the literature of marginalisation,
that metamorphoses into an alien tongue;
our metaphors, wandering ghosts of past lives.
Is this choice or *karmic* banishment
from the land of our dreams, with an
imagined Indianness? Exotic interpreters
of Shakespeare and Browning, we are
the new academia, the new pedagogues
of the West, a brave new breed
that even Macaulay dare not minute.

MARGINAL OR PERIPHERAL

How can I celebrate being British
and multicultural when the students
I teach mimic my accent in hyperboles?
Am I marginal or peripheral?

Now the periphery invades the centre
and rewrites history in smudged margins,
like mischievous schoolboys, who abuse
their teachers in obscene drawings
on the margins of dog-eared exercise books
and on the dark walls of their adolescent minds.

Am I the intellectual, teaching Victorian
poetry and Dracula's otherness to
Christianity, translating Caliban's tongue
to boisterous teenagers, who read meaning
in my words and in the colour of my skin?

I live on the edge of history and politics,
wallowing in the culture of a distant
monsoon land. Equality is new rain, here.
I breathe in the old rain, the latticed
winds of racism and anti-racism.
In swirling mists, I recall grimaces,
harsh words and jibes reserved
only for the marginal and the peripheral.

Now the periphery takes up arms:
guerrilla warfare of equality
in bullet points, marginal aesthetics
of resistance in *Bhangra* dances
and subterranean poetry
in gender coded interlanguage.

IN EXILE

After Naomi Shihab Nye

Language is the magic carpet
of their exile. Strolling the streets
of London in alien garb, as striking
as the Himalayan tiger-sky,
they laugh like *koels*, calling
across the Ganges spring.
Summered plains flower
on their silken *kameezes*,
tasselled with golden beads
that light the dwindling dusk,
like embroidered glow worms.
When dark wintering suns haunt
the skies and rain falls forever,
they see peacock visions dancing
under lightning clouds
and long for hot *pakoras*
and *masala* tea to spice up
their monsoon dreams.

EAST LONDON

From the cascading sounds of cityscape,
a familiar tune flows out of a passing car –
Hayo Rabba, Hayo Rabba, Hayo Rabba
– and soars past the smoky grey lines
of old terraced houses, wedged
between new glass monuments,
aspiring Taj Mahals of the 21st century.
Winding my way through a maze
of languages – Hindi, Bengali, Tamil,
Urdu, Malayalam – I trespass
on bold immigrant dreams.
Cutting across spiced *souks*, I seek
the ambience of mosaic territory,
sans nations, *sans* borders, *sans* disputes.
An old church, converted into a temple tower,
drones in *mantras*, rising on the filigreed wings
of exiled visions. I am bathed in the milk
of Sanskrit, clothed in divine raiment, perfumed
by incense and camphor, drowned in soliloquies
of pealing bells. A handsome young god,
alighting on peacock-back, welcomes me
with open arms: *Yamirukka bhayamen?*
Why fear when I am here?

JALLIANWALA BAGH

This is a garden of remembrance, of a harvest festival,
sanctified by the blood of patriots, who sleep like
unanswered prayers under the arc of a stoic sky.
From the well that drowned their cries of nation
and freedom, they shall rise again. Embedded on
the walls, bullet scars; unforgiving tales of an empire,
whose sun had to set in the east. Infant angels hover
around the well, as a lofty monument meditates
in the pale wintry light. An eternal flame burns
at the portal: converging, diverging, rekindling.
A century passes, debating on inhuman history,
brutal gleaning and fiendish firepower. Dare I question
the unrepentant empire? The old mosque, on the side,
kneels down, thanking the martyrs in five prayers.

DOPPELGÄNGER

After the film Paheli*, dir. Amor Palekar*

Rising lithely from the lilting rhythms
                                        of dancing marionettes,
you swirl smoothly   into the sandscape
                                        in sagas of silvered smoke.
In the whimsical wings of the west, you tread
                                the sharp ooze of burning sun.

A shadow creature wandering across myths,
a banished soul   without a name.
Your breath, a prayer to the sky,
                                        your skin, the desert air.

A nomad, you wrap the golden dunes
like a turban   around your head,
                                only your moustache is conjured up.

On starlit nights, refrains sifting the singing sands,
                                                you croon to the moon.
You frisk and frolic   by the fireside,
where women whirl in the wind,
their bangles chasing fireflies, their veils trailing
                                                your eidolon visions.

In your spectral mind, strange affections grow tender,
an uncanny longing   to paint the drifting ergs
with ethereal mirages refracting
                                the myriad moods of love.

Legends draw a thin line
between life and death,
old shepherds' tales bearing
the pregnant reveries of your earth woman.

When camel caravans draw in the dawn,
like a delectable dream,
a doe-eyed beauty haunts your phantom heart
in the red-wingèd song of the bush lark.

ON THE FIRST READING OF BRAM STOKER'S *DRACULA*

Uncle Narayan's tall, dark bookcase looms large
against the grey stone wall; its antique mahogany

frame oozes forlorn elegance; its gothic arches touch
the sky; its scalloped shelves conceal decadent caches

behind leaded glass doors. At fifteen, I am a wanton
juvenile frequenting this fairy realm, this leather-bound

wordsmith world that draws me into twilight trysts.
A bearded Irishman stares back at me from a dust jacket,

wonder man, artful spinner of nebulous yarns that surpass
grandmother's *Yakshi* and *Gandharva* tales. A wilful

romance flutters in from an unknown land, camouflaging
a Cimmerian legend that would haunt my nights in wolves,

bats and fangs. As I turn the pages, I am possessed
by a saturnine spirit that relentlessly preys on women.

Night after night, a restless creature stalks my thoughts
as I lie in bed shivering, windows shut tight and bolted

with garlic; a borrowed crucifix from the convent,
threaded to my rosary of *tulsi* beads; hidden under

my pillow, a tiny brass phial of saffron, infused with
the powers of Kali, dark talisman of light. I gaze dazedly

through the skylight, at the pale monsoon moon, oblivious
that my midnight horror fancies would soon shape-shift

into Christopher Lee and in years to come, bedevil my
classrooms, brimming with wide-eyed teenagers, in a wild

wayward genre of bloody imaginings, *Schauerroman*,
otherness to Christianity and a coven of fantastical creatures

that shook the very pillars of the ubiquitous British Empire.
As I gingerly re-entomb the nefarious book in its glass crypt,

my wingèd childhood fears assume a liminal form.

FISH AVATAR

When the great deluge began, your eternal form
rebirthed in water, generating flood legends
that swam across centuries. Gills breathing in
stars, suns, moons, comets and all, in whirling
cycles of creation and uncreation; hungry mouth
recycling the waters of the sky, you slew conch
demons, rescued infant *Vedas*, tied serpent ropes
to the seeded wooden arks of patriarchal flood heroes,
dragging them across swelling seas, anchoring them
on promontories poised on the edge of epochs.
Through eons, streamlined body inhaling and exhaling
the fire of time, you crawled on all fours, from fish
to tortoise to boar to half-man, half-beast and came
to a grinding halt by divine decree. Your universal form,
zoomorphic, hallowed by wingèd myths, stretches
across space, waiting for man to evolve; while
light-years below you, the womb of patient earth
pulses with teeming streams of your celestial seed.

TEACHING TAGORE TO 10A/S

Who wanders high on the palace-tower, hair unravelled, unravelled
Pulling her cloud-blue sari
Close to her breast?
Who gambols in the shock and flame of the lightning, O who is it
High on the tower today with hair unravelled?
– 'New Rain' by Rabindranath Tagore, translated from Bengali by William Radice

Tagore drizzles mistily on 10A/S, as my dusky
voice trembles in the monsoon winds; it is
tossed across the stillness of the room, stifling
questioning looks; it strikes the walls, its duskier
echoes rumble in the corners; flickering curiosity
sparks and lights, gathering interest soaks the air
and scattered smiles seep into the room.

Floating an Indian poet in an English class,
enhanced by *sitar* music, to be tuned into ears
overflowing with Anglic notes and Saxon beats,
seemed ridiculous at first; but with drumming
heart I read, with dancing eyes, they listen.

I, a relic of the Raj, token of the minority race,
clasp Tagore to my breast and attempt
multiculturalism, a gigantism, knocking at
the doors of sleepy classrooms, stumbling along
the corridors of waking schools, perching precariously
on the narrow shelves of dreamy stockrooms.

Kadamba trees blossom, *ketaki* trees gather moss,
bakul trees branch out into the wilderness,
as I wander among the desks, high on rhythm,
low in tone; flashes of doubt charge the air
as strange words and their stranger sounds
rain in torrents. Multiculturalism, with
a wry smile, thunders down.

Sitting cross-legged on the table, I watch
their eyes move softly across the page
and murmur Indian words, while my
thoughts drift back to that river bank,
where I left my water-pot and my heart.

I show them Tagore as a relief from Donne,
they find a brave new world of dreams
and songs. A hand shoots up: *'Asian women*
and hair unravelled? Reformation or rebellion?'

I remove my glasses from my eyes; the woman
in the poem is gone. I take her place: new rain
floods my being, rain clouds wet my eyes, as
Nazeem unveils the *purdah* of Indian womanhood.

IMMIGRANT

A country stretches across my wings,
at times a burden, at others a blessing.
I have learnt to live with it, its silhouettes

of waving palm fronds seizing my dreams,
its myths spreadeagled on my verse, the cry
of its peacocks, haunting my silent nights.

I feel its goddesses in the feminine flow
of my form, I whisper its twilight prayers
in my sleep. My country grows with its roots

penetrating my bones, it binds the culture
of distance into my heart. Its paraphernalia
of blue gods, red demons, sun festivals,

its skies screaming with the wild colour
of a thousand autumns and its aching moons
scatter my forlorn thoughts in desert storms.

Its laughing avalanches dissolve into the rivers
of my blood, its westerlies echo the swirling cadences
of my soul, adding yet another story to the history

of migrant birds. Time flies with me on the back
of a wingèd cloud and I wrap the retreating monsoons
around me, like a shimmering pashmina shawl.

I fly in monsoon skin that thunders in an alien sky.
Sharp shards of feathered lightning rend the new air.

SHIVA

Shiva, mythical model for deviant art, with leopard skin gear,
seed beads, crescent moon and crawling snake jewellery, you
are the almighty dude, the ultimate sensation, wearing woody

notes of camphor and aegle bark, distilled with *fougères* of
sandalwood and a lingering hint of *Nirvana*. A graphic half-
nude god posing demurely in an aureole of flames, a poster

icon, encapsulated in trilogies, muscles rippling, dreadlocks
flowing, mapping the world with trident and battle cries, you
sail down the flailing waves of time in history, myth and legend.

You have an uncanny forte for poising on one leg, your hour-
glass drum throbbing in cyclical timbre; with your legendary
addiction to cannabis, you flaunt an unerring penchant for luring

bevies of beauties: Parvati, Dakshayani, Kamakshi, Ganga.
You are the half-woman god of TV serials, gyrating across starry
nights, a phallic symbol overflowing with untamed primal energy.

Wrapping the sky around your slim waist, you fall into dance,
trance and ecstasy; sexual asceticism, your way of life.
Vibrating to the yogic breath of sound and silence, you create

the world in cosmic union with Shakti, in a wave of light dancing
in primordial harmony on the walls of an expanding universe.
Atop a snow-clad Tibetan mountain, you deliberately discount

politics, devour time and dream the world for aeons with shut eyes,
only to burn it down in wilful gusto with the convenient fire
of your third eye. Your unforeseen shape-shifting into a dragon-

headed, lion-taming monster deity, inspiring awe even among
aghori sadhus, who plait rivers into their hair. As Pashupati,
lord of beasts, your ambitious odyssey spans uncharted space,

where no god has gone before. In vibrant blue CGIs, you board
a light propelled UFO, in some virtual world of gods and demons,
poising your nuclear warheads at the end of lightning arrows.

With subtle panache, you take aim from Pinaka, that fiery,
self-willed bow. In atomic precision, in finesse and in fire,
you shoot down the three-tiered, metal-clad, hellish satellite city

orbiting the earth and lithely pirouette to celestial rhythms
that echo across the maze of pulsing galaxies:
Shiva Sankara, Shiva Sankara, Shiva Sankara…

IMMIGRANT TEXT

You are another immigrant banter:
postcolonial, subversive, reactionary.
You are an ageless debate, a shift
of paradigm, an appropriation
of language, an in-between space.
You are a quicksilver text, wilful
and bold one moment, fragile
and fading the next. You are
a centripetal force, spinning away
from the galaxy of mainstream texts,
lingering in the peripheries, wanting
to be read, but your phrases are flat
and unanchored, your metaphors
hang in the air, your images are
overworked and stretch to create
a countercurrent. Your rhetoric
is formulaic, your argument
dominates form, and there
is an ironic juxtaposition
of assimilation and marginalisation.

I can see what you are trying to say.
I am you and you are me, between us,
we could be the wild exotic extracting
anti-imperial dreams from dark nights
and dragon wings; we could be comets
dreaming of new freedom, the freedom
of being read, of being understood.

MEN IN TURBANS

Few people are aware 1.5 million Indians fought alongside the British – that there were men in turbans in the same trenches as the Tommies.
–Shrabani Basu

Forgotten
by the world,
we linger in no man's land.
Forsaken by history,
trampled by time,
renounced by a homeland
that does not honour
its imperial troops.

Our dreams lie scattered
across the Western Front;
our blood spilt in vain,
our memories fragmented
by empire, colony and nation.
Our lives, a redundant sacrifice
for *king and another country*.

Wear your poppies with pride,
but tell us who we are:
Brown *sepoys* of the Raj
or comrades, who fought
arm in arm, losing eye and
limb, when cannons roared
like thunder and bullets
hurtled like rain?

REFUGEE CHILD

Old words translate
into new words like
stars that fit

into his night brain
each word is a star
lighting his new world

its light drifting
in the mind muddled
by murky depths

that swallowed
some of him
in its angry mouth

he is a blue child
who came out of the sea
in an orange dream

he looks around for ghosts
that followed him
through hellfire and deluge

he translates the moon
Qamar – the drowned face
hanging in the sky

he mutters prayers
for his helplessness
his sin of survival

like the moon
he has a dark face
the one he hides

THE JABBERWOCK REPLIES

I was whiffling through the tulgey wood,
when he discovered me, with nonsense verse
and redundant spells. He then stitched me up
in a flighty tale about this dippy reptilian foe,
waiting to be slaughtered by a spirited gallant,
brandishing a vorpal blade that went snicker-snack.
What did he take me for? The Lambton Worm?

By the way, it is never brillig in the wabe
and when I am around, the slithy toves
dare not gimble, dare not gyre.
The mome raths are such sloths
that they cannot possibly outgrabe.
Speaking of the borogoves, they are neither
mimsy nor momsy; hare-brained creatures,
sleeping by day and scavenging by night.

Jubjub bird is a ridiculous sobriquet
for Garuda, serpent slayer, king of birds,
his great wings chanting the *Vedas* in flight.
And frumious Bandersnatch is a crass epithet
for Hanuman, mighty monkey god, who
wrestles with demons and leaps across seas,
setting vile island-kingdoms ablaze
with a swish of his swirling tail.

And what bizarre rubric for the world tree?
The tree of life, on which Odin relentlessly
sacrificed himself, hanging for nine days
and nine nights. Can you even imagine?
The Sacred Ash, Yggdrasil, with branches

in the heavens and roots in the netherworld,
re-christened Tumtum tree?

As for Beamish boy, he is no St. George,
no Merlin's minion, wielding the Excalibur.
He is an altogether preposterous fop,
day-dreaming of snatching damsels
from the flaming mouths of dragons.
Spurned by women, he drowns his sorrows
in vinous spirits and never, ever galumphs.

It makes me chortle in sneer, to think
that the feather-brained old man caloohed
and callayed at that jaded dragon mask
Beamish produced; its beady eyes
dripping with phosphorescent paint.

THE ENGLISH PATIENT TRANSLATES DESERT LIGHT

After Michael Ondaatje

The English patient inhales the oasis in his dreams
and drinks the liquid air. Embalmed on his altared bed,
he relishes the reveried reading of the nurse, the gaps
in the narrative throwing twilight shadows that dance
on the maimed ceiling. He swallows her words
like wine and plucks his *simsimiyya* heart for notes
that soar on falcon wings. In the distance, he hears
the high-pitched bark of a fennec fox, the clipped cry
of a flamingo in flight. He wears his indigo face
like an eclipsed sun; a river lost among sandstorms,
he is masked in reeds that filter the moon to soothe
his burning skin, his antlered head of fire. He hovers
above the drifting ergs, where wandering *djinns*
had bewitched his plane. He moves in his sleep,
trading fragrance and spice across *bedouin* routes,
north of Giza, where archangels alight on crystal wings.
He translates ghost light that wades across the sand
and drowns in a cave of swimmers. Cloistered in
a battered nunnery, upon a besieged Italian hill,
he chants the names of winds: *haboob*, dressed
in golden robes, carrying rain; *harmattan*, howling
across the Sahara, a red wind cloaked in night;
simoom, dark dawn swirling in tawny cloud, engulfing
whole armies in its wake. By day, he decodes desert
light in a language not his own. At night, when all
is quiet, he unravels light in his own tongue, rising
on the redolent wings of *datoo*, a westerly that seeks
an imagined heaven; a camel caravan, flowering
date palms and an enchanted oasis of little birds.

PONDICHERRY

A boulevard town, union territory,
La Côte d'Azur de l'Est, enclave
of the French East India company,
once split into *Ville Blanche*
and *Ville Noire*; the colours
now erased by saffron and green.
Passing through the centuries
into a courtyard of history,
retaining the borders
of French India, the city
soaks in the sun that frolics
on its endless beaches,
Promenade, Paradis, Sérénité;
a literary niche for fantasy genres
of marooned tigers and palaces
of chocolate melting
into the Indian summer.
Only the language lingers in the *rues*,
gendarmes and *le Foyer du Soldat*,
filtering into my verse through Mahé
in the Kerala coast. The World War I
memorial on Beach Road meditates
at the crossroads of nations:
Aux combattants
des Indes Françaises
morts pour la patrie.
I stand under Gandhi's stony resolve
and Aurobindo's spiritual aura;
both meeting at two distant points
of enlightenment, holding
tension in the concept of *liberté*,
each proclaiming: *Je est un autre*.

PARTITION 1947

Partition is central to modern identity in the Indian subcontinent, as the Holocaust is to identity among Jews, branded painfully onto the regional consciousness by memories of almost unimaginable violence.
– William Dalrymple

this subcontinent is a nation no more no more it is a wretched body
of broken bones flesh gut and blood spilling across railway tracks
across wine red seas across the politics of deceit across a faraway
island that ruled the seas tired of divisions tired of being slaves
of a stepmother nation that ruled land sea and sky an island nation
showered by the curses of its colonies that trembled under its foot
curses showered by centuries that quaked under the roar of its cruel
cannons under its consummate brute desire to conquer the world

this subcontinent is a nation no more no more its suicidal hands
slicing off its sea its land its sky mapping its own desires of self-rule
its terrors in the wake of its own reforms its fear of its thirty million
gods who metamorphosed into blood and gore its two-nation theories
that created more nations of discord among its heterogeneous races
its multifarious languages its nefarious rituals its bloodthirsty people
descending into chaos in a motherland torn apart by strife leaving a
million songs unsung a million tales untold a million dreams undreamt

this subcontinent is a nation no more no more its everlasting
mutinies its war mongering dynasties its power-hungry leaders
spawned by bigotry and animal passion all falling under the spell
of an island kingdom queen of all nations ruling the waves
this subcontinent its geographies marking its histories its languages
chronicling its cultures its blaspheming men raping its women
birthing a generation of bastards hacking a nation's breast splitting
open its womb this dark subcontinent is a broken down cannibalistic
goddess created by fair men with fairer dreams of a better world

for themselves in hill stations in summer capitals in a virgin land
that prostitutes itself to white masters a land of culture subjugating
itself to anarchy a land of peace opening itself to violence its hapless
female soul trapped between many libidinous male gods descendants
of some other sky who write a crazed and bloodied history on the
breast of time of myriad lives trampled in myriad border crossings

this subcontinent is a nation no more no more this subcontinent wallowing
in bloodbaths has no beginning no end its seething memories stretching
across the centuries a standing testament of imperial follies a distortion
of historical trajectories that eclipse nations making trysts with destinies
at midnight when the world sleeps this subcontinent will divide into two
its cities ablaze its furies unleashed smothering all sense and sensibility
shrinking its languages groping for lost words its soul weeping in funereal
silence on its maimed body a mutilated apology of a nation sowing seeds of
discord and the mother nation waging an inglorious war on its glorious Raj

this subcontinent is a nation no more no more it lies cowering
under the mantle of never ending night when wolves howl
when vultures tear open its guts when myths devour its children
when daybreak is a legend that dawns upon other skies
this subcontinent will weep until the end of time in blood
for tearing itself asunder like some monster child tired of its own
screams this subcontinent and its seismic shifts of ideologies
its vicious politics of partition defining the contours of its land
and sea defiling its people like a plague an eternal curse hangs
upon its people in the poignant cry of an old nation self-immolating
at the altar of freedom sometimes scarlet sometimes stygian
sometimes silver like lightning piercing the heart of a weeping sky

FUSSY MILITANT REBEL

You want me to be invisible.
I want to be seen. You preach
equality, but I want difference.
You call me fussy.

You want me to grin and bear
your affectionate connections
with the *Paki* corner shop.
I demand an apology.
You dub me militant.

You want me to nod assent
when you are rewarded
for my efforts. I ask
for acknowledgement.
You title me rebel.

I play by your rules,
but you call me names,
for I am your other; your
reflection in a dark mirror,
your consciousness in colour.
I am Caliban, you want to tame me,
I am the exotic, you want to taste me.
When I say I am human, like you,
you get lost in the dual labyrinths
of nature and culture.
I want to be seen!
I want to be heard!
I want to be thought of!

I demand non-stop.
I get my difference, my
apology, my acknowledgement!
Somewhere in you lurks
the *Sahib*; you very soon
give into the stubborn native
in me. Your atavistic guilt
would kill you otherwise.
Somewhere in me lurks
a spirit that haunts you
day in and day out.
My atavistic wounds
would not heal otherwise.

SOLITUDE

I do not live in loneliness   I live in solitude
When I look back   at the turn of the millennium
I am amazed   at a life lived in exile   a silken sash
of thoughts   stretches across this island   my new home
an island   within a bigger island   ruled by old gods
who travelled the seas   and colonised the world

my sea has no end   it flows out of cliffs   and touches the sky
I am monarch of all I survey   my solitude greater than Selkirk's
I live in words   in words that I read   in words that I write
in metaphors of exile   in allegories of solitude

I have given up fighting exile   I have befriended new gods
I have drunk new wine   tasted new bread   breathed new air
I seek no wings   I seek dreams   that fly in darkness
to keep promises   in light   old gods come back
to claim me   would they live in peace   with my new gods
Brahma, Vishnu and Shiva   meet   Manannan, Ymir and Venus

I am cast away   on this island   marooned by tides
from another life to here   on this beach   scattered with words
on this beach ebbing   in solitude   old moons wane
new moons wax   in newer light   silence melts into sand
I must walk this beach alone   new thoughts are born   new verse

UNDERSTANDING CALIBAN

You taught me language, and my profit on 't
Is I know how to curse. The red plague rid you
For learning me your language!
– *The Tempest*, Act I, scene ii

He wore his misery like a menacing sky;
his language a curse around his neck,
the colours of tempests seeping through
his eyes. He was a mooncalf, a beast
man, a freckled monster; an absent dream,
confined to a rock, with no spirit
to command. His isle of wonder,
full of noises, sounds and sweet airs,
where his master summoned many a storm.
Some called him *Kalee-ban*, satyr
of the dark goddess Kali. Others called
him the whelp of blue-eyed Sycorax,
who whored after the devil himself.

At a magical time past the mid-season,
he slipped out of the folio edition, lips
mumbling a prayer to Setebos, and ventured
out of his sea-sorrow into a new world
of brave imaginings. He became verse
that named the bigger light burning by day
and the smaller light burning by night.
He watched many a sunset, when sea and
sky went up in flames; he dreamt of new
beginnings, of brave gods, of celestial wine,
of stars that wove spider webs across the night.

He never returned to his folio, but split
himself in many forms, flaming amazement,
appropriating and burning in many places,
like Indra's lightning, precursor of dreadful
thunderclaps, far from momentary.
He sowed fiery metaphors into the crevices
of oceans, roaring with imperial visions.

A TRIBUTE TO M. F. HUSAIN

MOTHER INDIA

This is a flat planar nude of a nation;
a cavalier composition of a motherland
in cardinal red, the view of a 'graphics *wallah*'
on a bill board poster; a *tour de force* translation
of linear space and womanhood that lost
its harmony to a cacophony of death threats.
What I read is a vermillion woman, beautifully
proportioned like a Bollywood heroine,
willowy like a Kalidasa goddess. Her hair
flies into the Himalayas in the same shade
of red and contrasting white; it floats ribbon-
like into a candied sky, a river flowing back
to the mountains, where a strange sun sets
in childish glee. The length of her limbs
sinuous, serpentine, seductive, poised like
a *Bharatanatyam* dancer in frieze.
She is the synecdoche of the nation,
balancing the *ashoka chakra* like an infant
on her hips; a woman subverting aeons
of servitude in the names of states, calligraphed
on her bosom, her waist, her thighs, her feet,
around her navel. The dark space between
her slender form and the map abstracts
the pain of Indian womanhood, through his
bleeding chroma and wayward sensitivity.
Her yearning gaze towards a hermetic sky
compromises the half-lotussed, dark, male figure,
meditating on thirty-three million gods.

She is the woman behind the nation, a relic
of the future, breaking out of his flaming canvas;
a bold narrative beyond the rigid geometry
of perspective. Her veiled hands recede into
the past, holding like fire, an immigrant song.
She is a vision that forced herself on him; a surreal
spirit negotiating a half formed Arabian Sea
that trades in a catamaran of black and red.

M. F. HUSAIN'S GODDESSES

Your bohemian brushstrokes, caustic curves of breast,
limb and thigh, endorsed whiplash *art nouveau*
and violent hate campaigns. Your libertarian carnival
of voluptuous goddesses spreadeagled in iconographic
aesthetic ate into the very core of the snarled Indian psyche.

Spreading your contentious canvas on floors and walls,
you mixed Picasso and Cézanne into *Hindustani* matte.
Your full chroma of *Kufic Khat*, narrative cubism
and tantric mystique portrayed a Manichaean realm,
each contour, each impasto anchoring each nude goddess
in political chiaroscuro, a diptych of decadence and design.

Diaphanous divinities dancing in incandescent tonality,
denuded river deities flowing with fish, bare-breasted
supernal women riding on lions, chaste wives poised
on demon thighs and a female nation in flat planar nude,
all tumbled out of pictorial space, invading a land
of volatile gods. Your abstract altarpieces drew surreal ire,
your signature sketches of a cryptic elephant god tilted
celestial balance, arousing antiphonies of revolt and reverence.

Accused of blasphemy and betrayal, branded sinner
and saint, you fled into exile. Your raw interpretations
of eternal archetypes, dancing provocatively on temple murals,
embalmed your eccentric genius. Your dishabille portfolio
of divine form, profane polyphony and discerning rhythm –
a construct undefined, a dimension unseen, a clear cut
controversy in colour. Dangerous Art!

A TALE OF THREE CITIES

After Husain's triptych of the same name

DELHI

On an inchoate landscape, the parliament
of the largest democracy on earth spins,
a satellite of politics. In unbroken smudges
of monochromatic brown, in a shallow,
relief-like space, realigned forms evolve
into multiple vantage points. An unfurling flag,
bearing totems of dynasty rule, passes through
the faceless figure in a Nehru jacket.
Hominid faiths contour the chassis of the city
without walls. In the omphalos, a female
figure in a white sari brazenly exposes
her navel; womanhood in the making,
guarded by a single file of men, who seem
an afterthought. On a fragmented palimpsest,
a cognisant India Gate muses in eternal flame.
A multi-tiered capital, painted in layers of history.

BENARES

On a crimson sky, a recalcitrant monkey
flies over pinnacles of slanted temples
that metamorphose into a sculptural
half-woman god. On the *ghats*, a bisected
figure in yellow and brown dreams an elegy
under a rudimentary parasol; while two
angular women worship a ribbon

of blue, a river flowing in small joys
and sorrows through the interstitial spaces
of burghal anatomy. On a tilting boat,
a crow swings on an earthen pot, the reliquary
of an exiled artist. In the foreground, a grand
old man plays his clairvoyant *shehnai*,
summoning spirits in tangled geometry.
A transcendental Hindu monk diffuses
into the synthetic edges of the anterior panel
and Nandi, the overlapping sacred bull, discerns
the abstract precision of the city, older than
history, older than tradition, older than legend,
twice as old as all of them put together.

CALCUTTA

On the left, a bearded sage, askance,
serenades the scene in an advancing palette
of adjacent hues. Civil unrest and freedom fire
set alight by a bespectacled patriot, a chiaroscuro
saga of a heaving city; a vanishing point
at which the nation unfolds herself
in retrospect. In the shadows, an Albanian
nun rescues an abandoned child, and an ashen
rickshaw-wallah ambles along with a bulky
Bengali babu on his back. Winding his camera
through the meandering streets, a film-maker
contemplates its cultural *milieu* in black and white.
Banished to the background, the Victoria
memorial, a marvel of the past that forever
haunts the Indian psyche. A Bengal tiger roars
across your canvas invoking a dark goddess,
devourer of time, who mourns you in dance.

BOLLYWOOD ON THE UNDERGROUND

This size zero Bollywood belle
is a visual poem on the underground;
her eyes resting on *Skyfall*,
her feet on *shaadi.com*.
She is as lithe as a panther,
an alien animal unravelling you
with a smile. Lips parting in
Pre-Raphaelite seduction,
she poises between continents;
her hair cascading like the Ganges,
across time zones. Her toned abs
are a surreal notion, her upraised
breasts, an urban myth; her slender
thighs are a metrosexual fantasy;
her dainty waist, a latitude of desire;
her dusky skin, a dreamy abstraction.
With passing eyes drinking her
like wine, she is the Mona Lisa
of the Tube; her shapely hand
rising out of the wall, behind
the escalator, to touch you on
the shoulder, to rinse you in
an Indian summer, under
the domed subway sky.

INDO-PAK 2001

Here on this island, we get together and talk
of back home – Karachi, U.P., Lahore, Kerala.
Back home, you play war games, shake hands,
issue nuclear threats, deliver patriotic speeches;
religions must be appeased, regions contested,
elections won and the mass of humanity ignored.
We eat samosas, sip cold drinks and talk
of the British weather, Bollywood heroes
and Manx education, while our children scream
in the background. Being an exile is unique
indeed, even enemies become friends.
You dig trenches, exchange fire and call
each other names, you who were brothers,
now excel in the game of Abel and Cain.
We giggle at old photographs and reach out
for our lipstick-stained glasses, cluttering
the low table, unwittingly exchanging them.
There is no Hindu *paani* and Muslim *paani* here,
no watery grave that devours humanity.
You debate over the LoC that broke the land
and a million hearts; you carry out your suicide
missions. Your newspapers throw word-flares:
fragile, fuming, fiery, while your film industries
market: Hate Thy Neighbour.
We curse the partition, the prize-fighting, the
politics and watch the television in silence
as the British Prime Minister takes the hand
of history and flies to the subcontinent,
to undraw a line drawn by long ago.
Peace, to us, is a vision that rises from the East.
Peace, to you, is a line drawn by the West.

INDO-PAK 2016

A Celtic God covers this island
    with his misty cloak.
Maples bleed in red, cherry
    blossom in yellow,
as fleeing swallows twitter
    of looming war.
Across the horizons of time,
    Nehru and Jinnah
make pacts with freedom,
    and that grand old man
goes on hunger strike,
    satyagraha, desire for truth.
In Uri and Pathankot, across
    the border, fire serpents hiss.
On television, they invoke
    Brahmastra, forbidden
weapon, to erase both sides
    of the map. I have left
history behind, to seek some
    other migrant heaven.
In my English class, that cheeky
    Pakistani boy wants
to know the meaning
    of *dulce et decorum est*.

WE AIN'T NO MORE PAKI MATE

We ain't no more Paki mate   we are part and parcel
of this island's history   spread across its geography
Romanis, our *bhanjaras*   crossing continents
and languages, wandering   your world with songs
on their lips, our *lascars*   recruited to steer
your ships, our ayahs,   native nannies to *memsahibs*
our shampoo surgeons   washing royal hair
with spicy hands   launching Hindoostanee
coffee, only to be   forgotten by history.

We ain't no more Paki mate   our turbaned soldiers
pulled out of the North West Frontier   fighting in your
World War, dying   on bloodied poppy fields
in Flanders, unsung,   unglorified without
a single poppy   worn back home
or here, where you   celebrate Remembrance.

We ain't no more Paki mate   when you split one India
in two, we were all   plain Hindustani, natives
of the British Raj   whose sun set on our shores
our Hindi, Urdu and Punjabi   adding music to your dialects
our blue-collared workers   toiling in your factories
and textile mills, *desi* men   and women driving taxis
our *desi log* in pharmacies   dispensing your medicines.

We ain't no more Paki mate   our *desi* tycoons
in your poshest Kensington   wooing you in steel and style
our *desi* doctors   wandering the corridors
of your NHS, in A&E,   in Cardiology, delivering your
babies, saving your lives,   keepers of your island health
our brown bobbies in blue   serving in your forces

leading your MET,   in *apna* London, a desi mayor,
son of a bus driver   running the *sahib's* affair.

We ain't no more Paki mate   our *samosas* and *paneer*
lining the aisles   of Tesco and Waitrose
our heritage vegetables   *bhindi, baingan* and *karela*
piling in Birmigham   in Bradford, in Manchester
in Southall, in East London   our shops, blaring with
Bollywood songs, with rainbow *saris*,   swinging in the breeze,
our restaurants serving   *desi daru* and *desi khana*
catching flame across the world   as the Great British Curry.

We ain't no more Paki mate   our temples and mosques
spiring into your skies   fluttering with *namaz* and *mantra*
our *Bhangra* dances wooing   your *Eisteddfod*, our *desi*
movies bending it like Beckham   our *desi* writers walking away
with your awards, honoured by   Faber, Macmillan and Oxford,
our *desi* poets appropriating   your imperial tongue
our curried words   drifting through your aesthetics
our *desi* discipline   ruling your classrooms, teaching you
Shakespeare, waxing lyrical   on Browning and Tennyson
our *desi* scholars lecturing   you in all things postcolonial
prescribing creative writing   our Kalidasa, Tagore, Kazmi
and Kutti Revathi translated   into the *sahib's* tongue
our *desi* hearts beating   in tune to *God Save the Queen*.

THE RADCLIFFE LINE

I am going through this terrible job as fast as well as I can and it makes no difference because in the end, when I finish, they are all going to start killing each other anyway.
– Cyril Radcliffe, July 1947

He was the unbiased cartographer,
given five weeks to draw a line
in blissful ignorance of incompatible,
blood-thirsty gods and a divided
consciousness that forced an empire out.
An unlikely bidder assigned to saw
a nation in two, to draw a haphazard
Radcliffe Line, to haunt a subcontinent
until the end of time. He drew not
by insight, but by strife, overshadowed
by distrust, diktats of religion, scattered
princely states and war time debt.

How a barrister from Lincoln's Inn,
with no knowledge of the land
and its colours, could redraw a nation,
no one knew. On an outdated map,
he demarcated seas, rivers and
valleys of a country, he had never seen.
He earmarked cities, hanging on
the edge of conflict; he broke iced
mountain peaks into impasse
and imbroglio; he drew a frontier land
of life and death. The architect of
partition, he was the empire's avenger
on a nation, whoring after alien gods.

A tryst with destiny, a preliminary sketch
of the longitudes of war, a *de facto* line
defining neither nation. The line
reincarnating as a fragile ceasefire margin,
that moves to and fro, with glacier tilt,
political wrangling, night shelling,
infiltration across barbed wire fences,
searing salt marshes and singing deserts.

Only when the gates open at the border
do you see the writing on the wall,
unfolding ugly rivalries of one people,
sawn in two. Seventy years later,
beyond the Radcliffe Line, an enemy journal
earmarks me for the verse of the week.

GREAT BRITISH CURRY

Great British Curry, half-caste progeny of an empire,
anglicised avatar of *kari*, your Tamil mother sauce,
spicing up history's bland meats and soggy vegetables,
marinating an entire subcontinent impounded
by the British Raj. You are no bastard blend
of bygone flavours, claiming a Middle
English or French pedigree. You are a finger-
licking, delectable delight, sizzling with the essence
of roasted colonial cumin, cinnamon, clove,
cardamom and coriander, simmering in native
tamarind, tomato or sour cream, seasoned in storms.

Your mouth-burning, sense-stirring vindaloo avatar,
illicit strain of the sea-faring *carne de vinha d'alhos*,
wafting through my exiled spaces, so piquant that
my eyes water for hours. Many times removed from
your erstwhile Portuguese purées, you frequent
my culinary dreams, sprinkled with the sultriness
of Indian summers, smacking with wanderlust and
a desire to conquer the world in turmeric visions,
splattered on the mongrel recipe universe of the internet.

I am that castaway at your fragrant window, roaming
the earth in search of a home. Now that I have found you,
I will grind you into my home thoughts in the mortar
and pestle of guilt, at leaving a nation that is no longer mine.

WHERE DO I BELONG?

After reading Mahmoud Darwish

Where do I belong?
I have only memories
of where I think I belong.
I was born a woman
as every woman is born.
I was raised a woman
as every woman is raised.
Where I think I belong,
I have a house, but not
a home, not anymore.
Just north of my one-time
home, there is a shrine to her,
that dark woman I worshipped
at dawn and dusk. Then, there
are waving palm fronds that welcome
me as a prodigal daughter.
I am as all prodigals
are, a wanderer, an exile,
a migrant bird, a *khanabadosh*.
Hidden in the depths
of my metaphors are:
a demon king, a sleeping god
and a praying serpent.
I lived with them long before
I exiled myself. I belonged
there, when verse was birthed
by my mother. I have learned
all the words for verse, except
my own, that I betrayed
for the sake of an alien tongue.

I write in an alien tongue.
Here, they frown
at my Sanskrit similes,
they laugh at my exiled verse
and foreign rhymes. But I
cannot go back. I belong
here now, not there. I hang
on the perilous edge
of a monsoon cloud, to steal
a lightning quill, to write
my exiled dreams in rain and tears.
I know I am an exile;
I am an exile here,
an exile there, an exile
everywhere. Without
this exile, I am no one.

KALI

How can I portray you as a goddess here?
They would not comprehend your mini skirt
of severed arms, your garland of demon heads,
your serpent bracelets, your vicious fangs
and lolling tongue seeking some twilight vein,
your dishevelled hair flying across the world.
They would not decipher a vampire goddess,
holding a decapitated head, a skull bowl,
a bloodied scythe. They would not fathom
a terrible *tantric* deity, anklets ringing across
eternity, marrying the sacred and the profane.

Perhaps they would appreciate, if I portray
you as scantily clad, Third World feminist,
flagrantly flaunting comely breasts,
slender waist and shapely thighs; your lithe
body, dark as night, revelling in sensuality;
your red eyes, as inebriate as the wine you
constantly consume. They would possibly
envisage you as polymorphous primeval energy,
devouring time in flickering tongues of flame;
female wrath trampling male divinity, inhabiting
the fringes of liminal nature; woman boldly
crossing boundaries, eluding all definition.

NIKHAT'S MOTHER

She stands out in a crowd.
Her shocking pink
dupatta carrying
songs from the Gilgit.

She is without
a language here.
I am her interpreter,
translating her language,
her culture, her colour.

She does not understand
why Nikhat has to attend
school every day – *Nikhat*
is at her sister-in-law's
cousin's wedding
in Bradford.
Today is Mehndi,
Tomorrow is Nikah,
Day after is Walima.
Nikhat will not be in
school for a week.

She does not understand
why Nikhat is harassed
by school bobbies:
Bibi jaan, taleem lena,
dena hamara mamla hai.
Ye gore kyun dakl dete hain?

I interpret to the irate
Head of School –
Nikhat's mother does not
understand the concept
of compulsory education.

TRANSLATOR

To Ralph T. H. Griffith

Something breathed windless in twilight realms,
when you translated into occidental paradigm,
exotic cosmogonic myths that inscribe the truth
of the universe in daring pronouncements of earth,
water, fire, air and sky. Lyric summoning must have
roused your heart to the mystic beads of oriental thought,
sewn on the early fabric of time. A poet, you churned
your heart in metaphor and metonym to decipher
the might of *Vedic* gods. In the exquisite folds
of the nascent earth, when the eulogies of men touched
the skies and the guardians of the world smote the air
in white lightning, there must have been a desire within,
a seed of the eternal mind planted in imagined fragments,
which augured your words that rained down,
like a cosmic river from empyrean heights, with twin
moons for breasts, sun for smile and virginal might.
Frequenting the altars of myth, magic and incantatory rhyme,
you synchronised an inherent cultural otherness.
Cadenced in altered runes, your verse bequeathed
a cherished inheritance to the world. Into the warp
and weft of Sanskrit hymn, you wove in interlanguage,
intricate strands of oneiric spells, calling upon the sea
to swallow the sky, evoking spirits in funeral song,
conjuring occult charms to tame passing storms, invoking
dark-hued insatiate deities, cloaked in night's dusky raiment,
to sprinkle your staves with flaming refrain. Your decoded
strains cascade down the trail of centuries, shadow-playing
with forces of darkness, drinking libations of light,
wielding blazing thunder, speaking in parables to synods
of dreamers, igniting their visions with syllabic fire.

GOD OF MANY NAMES

Akashat patitam toyam yatha gachati sagaram
Sarva deva namaskarah kesavam pratigachati

O God of Many Names,
Are you not One?
I see you with many eyes,
Blinding my true eye.
Travelling through light,
I lose myself in darkness.
To realise One Truth,
I seek many falsehoods.
In your name, I burn down
All I had built through
The centuries.
In your name, I differ.
In your name, I disagree.
In your name, I destroy.
O God of Many Names,
Are you not One?

WALKING THE PROMENADE

Walking the promenade
is a ritual for us islanders.
We walk fastened
to our individual worlds,
humming the notes
of our recurrent dreams.
Earth forces hold us
down to the concrete,
often washed by the sea,
that changes with
the moods of the sky.
Twilight tide throws
wisps of seaweed
on the shore,
exiles like me.
Behind me, the hills
sing an old song,
as the roads curve
in and out
of the terrain,
like lines of verse
running on a page.
The sea merges
with my blood,
cascades through
my heart, plays with
my emotions that float
as lightly on air as on water.
Overhead, translating rock
and shell, heady seagulls
wing their desires.

Across the emerald bay,
flowing with my thoughts,
dancing on the waves,
a ferry crosses the mind.

CHANTING THE *VEDAS*

I chant the *Vedas*, I invoke a Dawn
Goddess, who unveils her bosom
unabashedly to the Sun God.
Named after her, every morning,
I chant a woman *mantra* to an alien sun.
I do not understand the essence
of my chant, but I close my eyes
to its music. When the sun rises
each morning, he tells me that I have been
anointed in the waters of the Ganges, that
I have reincarnated as sinless woman.
I have reincarnated into another,
so gradually, that I didn't even realise,
until my own gods spoke to me
in an alien tongue. I do not know
which of my gods touched my closed palms
and bequeathed exile, where I flounder
in lost womanhood, with *sindoor* bleeding
from my forehead. *Vedas* are a distant
soundtrack woven into my mind
that not even new verse can erase; a ghost
narrative that haunts me day in and day out.

FIRE *MANTRA*

My grandfather
taught me *mantras*
that I fell into, like *ghee*

offered at the bird altar,
where the noumenon
of fire awaits sacrifice.

I close my eyes and meditate
until fire draws me
inwards, into the altar of self.

Aham Vaishvanara, I am fire.
In my dreams, I trickle into
that fire, into the altar of self,

into *atman*, immortal soul. I travel
back in time; there is a fire
altar at the threshold of the old house,

where a blind old man sits
murmuring solemnly to Agni,
fire god. Behind me are all the *mantras*

I learnt, piling like firewood,
waiting to claim me.

NOTES

Immigrant traces the history, culture and languages of the British South Asians. The interlanguage used in this book is a mix of many languages of the Indian subcontinent and the colonial tongues of French and Portuguese. Many of these languages are spoken and used by South Asian immigrants living in the UK.

Khanabadosh: Urdu for nomad, my metaphor for diasphoric communities

Manasarovar: translated from Sanskrit as Mind Lake, is a freshwater lake on the Trans-Himalayan Tibetan plateau. Resting on the foot of Mount Kailas (Gang Rinpoche), the lake is associated with Indo-Tibetan myths and religious beliefs.

Yantras and *mandalas*: symbols and diagrams used in Hindu and Buddhist religious art

Chakora: Sanskrit for Indian partridge

Malayali: native of the Southern Indian state of Kerala and speaker of the Malayalam language

Indra: Indian equivalent of Jupiter

Vajra: Sanskrit for thunderbolt

Macaulay: Thomas Babington Macaulay's 'Minute' or memorandum on Indian education in the British Raj, 1835

Koel: Hindi for cuckoo

Kameez: Urdu/Hindi for tunic

Hayo Rabba: popular Punjabi song by the Bhangra legend Daler Mehndi

Yamirukka bhayamen: Tamil for 'Why fear when I am here'

Jallianwala Bagh: a garden in Amritsar, India, which witnessed great tragedy during the British Rule. On the 13th of April 1919, during the harvest festival of *Baisakhi,* troops of the British Indian army fired on peaceful protesters, killing more than 1000 people, including women and children. In panic, many protesters jumped into a nearby well and drowned.

Paheli: translated from Hindi as 'riddle', a Bollywood fantasy romance

Yakshi, Gandharva: In Indian folklore, *Yakshi* is a female vampire and *Gandharva* is a mythical male creature that seduces virgins.

Rosary of tulsi beads: a rosary made out of the wood of the basil (*tulsi*) plant

Kali: literally translated from Sanskrit as 'black', 'time' and 'death'; Kali is a Hindu goddess, legendarily associated with the slaying of demons and the destruction of evil.

'Fish Avatar' is based on the Indian flood myth, where the Hindu god Vishnu, in the form of a fish, rescued Manu (the Indian version of Noah) and the knowledge texts (*Vedas*) from the great deluge.

Vedas: *Ved* is Sanskrit for knowledge. The *Vedas* are a large body of Indian knowledge texts and are considered the oldest texts in Sanskrit and the oldest scriptures of Hinduism.

Sitar: a plucked string instrument used in Hindustani classical music

Kadamba, ketaki and bakul trees: These trees are all native to South Asia. Kadamba (*Neolamarckia cadamba*), evergreen tropical tree with perfumed flowers; ketaki (*Pandanus odorifer*), an aromatic screw pine; bakul (*Mimusops elengi*), a medium-sized evergreen tree with fragrant flowers.

Shiva: one of the principle deities of Hinduism, associated with the destruction of evil

'Shiva': the vibrant blue CGIs in the poem are a reference to Amar Chitra Katha's animated mythical film *Tripura, The Three Cities Of Maya*.

Simsimiyya: Arabic traditional plucked lyre

Pondicherry: formerly part of French India, Pondicherry is now a union territory, along with the other South Indian French enclaves of Karaikal, Yanam and Mahé. Pondicherry still retains its French characteristics in the use of language. *Le Foyer du Soldat* is a heritage monument in Pondicherry. It was the legion hall for retired French Indian soldiers. Erected in 1937, the war memorial in Pondicherry reads: *Monument aux combattants des Indes Françaises morts pour la patrie* (Monument to the soldiers of French India, who died for their country).

Je est un autre: 'I is another' – the words of the French poet Arthur Rimbaud in a letter to Georges Izambard, 1871

'Partition 1947': is inspired by William Dalrymple's article, 'The Great Divide' on the partition of India, 1947 (*The New Yorker*, June 2015)

Kalee-ban: 'Historical Contexts', *Shakespeare's Caliban: A Cultural History*, from Alden T. Vaughan, Virginia Mason Vaughan, Cambridge University Press, 1993

M. F. Husain (1915-2011): the grand old man of contemporary Indian art, a painter of great eminence and controversy. His paintings of Hindu goddesses and a nude Mother India elicited a hate-campaign by fundamentalist groups, following which Husain left India in 2006 to live as a self-exile in Dubai, Doha and London, where he died in 2011. The three poems 'Mother India', 'M. F. Husain's Goddesses' and 'A Tale Of Three Cities' are part of my ekphrastic work on Husain's paintings.

Ashoka Chakra: the wheel of Ashoka, depicted on the Indian flag

Hindustani/Hindostanee: Urdu for Indian

Kufic Khat: Oldest calligraphic form of Arabic scripts

Tantric: English adjective derived from the Sanskrit *tantra*, which is a Hindu and Buddhist ritualistic practice

Ghats: Anglicised plural of the Hindi *ghat*, a series of steps leading down to a river

Shehnai: a South Asian Indian (musical) wind instrument

Babu: Bengali/Hindi for gentleman

'A Tale of Three Cities': '(Benares is) older than history, older than tradition, older even than legend and looks twice as old as all of them put together' – Mark Twain

shaadi.com: Indian matrimonial website

Indo-Pak: a short form of India-Pakistan, a term used in the media and political circles

Paani: water. One of the 'divide and rule' policies of British officials in India, where the Muslims and Hindus were allocated segregated water taps.

LoC: Line of Control that divides India and Pakistan

Brahmastra: (*Brahma*: the Hindu creator god Brahma; *astra*: Sanskrit for weapon) in ancient Sanskrit writings, *Brahmastra* is considered the most destructive weapon, created by Brahma.

Bhanjara: Hindi for gypsy/nomad

Lascar: sailor or soldier from South Asia (from the Arabic word for guard or soldier, *al-askar*)

Ayah: Indian nanny employed by British families

Desi: collective term for people, culture and products of the Indian subcontinent or their diaspora (from *desh*, the Sanskrit word for land or country)

Log: Hindi/Urdu for people

Apna: Hindi/Urdu for 'our'

Paneer: Indian cheese

Daru: Hindi/Urdu for alcohol/spirit

Khana: Hindi/Urdu for food

Namaz: Muslim prayer

The Radcliffe Line: the boundary between India and Pakistan which took effect on 17 August 1947, during the partition of India. Named after its architect, Sir Cyril Radcliffe.

Kari: Tamil for curry sauce

Carne de vinha d'alhos: Portuguese for 'meat in garlic wine marinade'. The Portuguese colonised parts of the Central Indian coast, Goa, Daman and Diu. The Indian dish vindaloo is a derivative of the Portuguese *carne de vinha d'alhos*.

Dupatta: Hindi/Urdu for veil/scarf

Gilgit: a city in Northern Pakistan and is the gateway to the Karakoram ranges of the Himalayas

Mehndi: The henna ceremony before marriage; *nikah*: Muslim wedding ceremony; *walima*: reception

'Nikhat's Mother': The Urdu dialogue can be translated as: 'Madam, education is our personal business, why are the whites interfering?'

'Translator': Ralph Thomas Hotchin Griffith (1826-1906) was a scholar of Indology and Sanskrit, and translator of the *Vedas* into English.

'God of Many Names': The Sanskrit quote *'Akashat patitam toyam yatha gachati sagaram/ Sarva deva namaskarah kesavam pratigachati'* is from the Hindu *Sandhyavandhana*, or Twilight Prayer, and can be translated as: 'Every drop of water that falls from the sky goes to the ocean. Prayers offered to all Gods go to Kesava (the one God).'

Sindoor: (from the Sanskrit *sindooram*), a red cosmetic powder

Aham Vaishvanara: translated from Sanskrit as 'I am fire.' *Vaishvanara* is translated literally from the Sanskrit as the universal man (*vishva*: universe; *nara*: man). The reference here is to the *Rig Veda*, where Vaishvanara is an epithet of the fire deity Agni. It can also be interpreted as the fire within or fire of the soul.

Atman: Sanskrit for soul or inner self

Agni: Hindu fire god

ACKNOWLEDGEMENTS

I have many dues to pay. Where do I begin, where do I end?

Acknowledgements are made to the editors of the international journals and anthologies where earlier versions of many of these poems were first published: *Asia Literary Review, Bare Fiction Magazine, eSkylark, Fire, Index on Censorship, International Forum for Literature and Art, Kavya Bharati , Mascara Literary Review, Message in a Bottle, Muse India, Poetry Salzburg Review, The Redbeck Anthology of British South Asian Poetry, South Asian Ensemble, The Dance of the Peacock, The French Literary Review, The Hans India, The Missing Slate. Writing in Education, The Taj Mahal Review, Under the Radar.*

'Teaching Tagore to 10 A/S' was featured in the Tagore Centenary Project London Tagore Centre, 2001; 'I am Not One, but Two' and 'God of Many Names' were part of the German Translation project, Indische Gedichte und Geschichten, and translated into German by Johannes Beilharz and published in Stuttgart 2006; 'Fussy Militant Rebel' was part of a UK education project, conducted by Index on Censorship, 2005.

Thanks to the judges, who placed my poetry in the Ottakar and Faber Poetry Regional, Erbacce International Poetry Pamphlet; the Gregory O'Donoghue and the Exiled Writers Ink Poetry competitions. I am grateful to Culture Vannin (Isle of Man) for the publishing grant awarded towards this book.

I am grateful to the Word Masala Foundation and Yogesh Patel for the Word Masala Award in 2016 and for facilitating a reading at the House of Lords. I thank Todd Swift for that jaw-dropping wildcard announcement at the House of Lords in June 2016 and Eyewear Publishing for accepting my collection. I thank Jennifer Langer, the organiser of the Exiled Writers Ink Competition (2014), the first prize in which enabled me to get the Literary Consultancy Mentorship award. I thank Aki Schilz, Peter Forbes, Moniza Alvi and the Poetry School for their advice on my work.

I wholeheartedly thank my editor Alexandra Payne for her critical reading and advice. I thank Bashabi Fraser, Debjani Chatterjee, Jaydeep Sarangi and Sunil Sharma for their unflagging support. Many thanks to the Isle of Man Poetry Society, Jeff Garland and Janet Lees. Huge thanks to Mona Dash for a listening ear, a patient shoulder and a roof over my head, when in London for poetry readings. Finally, and most importantly, I thank Kishore, Smrithi and Shruthi for their tolerance and patience towards a forever writing wife and mother.